You Might Be a Cowgirl If ...

You Might Be a Cowgirl If ...

☆ ☆ ☆ **A GUIDE TO LIFE ON THE RANGE** ☆ ☆ ☆

Jill Charlotte Stanford

Photographs by Robin L. Corey

TWODOT®

GUILFORD, CONNECTICUT
HELENA, MONTANA
AN IMPRINT OF GLOBE PEQUOT PRESS

A · T W O D O T® · B O O K

Text design/layout: Lisa Reneson, TwoSisters Design
Project editor: Ellen Urban

Library of Congress Cataloging-in-Publication Data is available on file.

ISBN 978-0-7627-7809-6

Printed in the United States of America

10 9 8 7 6 5 4 3 2 1

This book is dedicated to

DALE EVANS

1912–2001

"The Queen of the Cowgirls"

*Cowgirl is an attitude really. A pioneer
spirit, a special American brand of courage.
The cowgirl faces life head-on, lives by
her own lights, and makes no excuses.
Cowgirls take stands; they speak up.
They defend things they hold dear.*
—Dale Evans Rogers, Los Angeles, 1992

The Roy Rogers Children's Trust

I'd Like to Be a Cowgirl*

I'd like to be a cowgirl
Ridin' the rodeo . . .
Fancy vest, leather chaps & boots with silver toes!

I'd like to be a cowgirl!
I'd trade my buttons & bows
For a name like Annie Oakley that everybody knows!

With my lasso quick and heavy . . .
I'd pull that critter down . . .
Then slap his hip with a Bar-C Brand
And head on into town!

I'd like to be a cowgirl!
That's the life that appeals to me!
Hoot and a Holler! Earn my silver dollar!
Singin' Yodel-lay-dee-tee!

* Music and lyrics by Rhonda Whiting, performed by the Sisters of the Silver Sage

CONTENTS

THANK YOU . . .

It has been a pleasure to write this book, largely because of the cowgirls that I can count on as my friends. They heard the call, saddled right up, and galloped to help me, no questions asked. I'm thankful for:

☆ Erin Turner, my editor at TwoDot Books, who was enthusiastic from the beginning;

☆ Robin Corey's beautiful photos, which grace this book and make it "real";

☆ Nancy Becker's vision of what Cowgirl True stands for, which I'm proud to include;

☆ Jan Mendoza's quick response and great examples;

☆ Cindy Hooker, who apparently wore her vintage boots as she wrote her "Minding the Herd" piece;

☆ Jamie Rauch, who was a godsend for the "Rodeo Queen" chapter!;

☆ All the rodeo queens who proved they were royalty by graciously answering my questions within twenty-four hours, even though they were out on the road, representing their rodeos;

☆ Sally Bishop, Patti Johnson, and Mary Roberts, who put their natural modesty aside and agreed to be role models for the cowgirl way;

☆ The Sisters of the Silver Sage, who wrote the perfect song and then shared it;

☆ Kate Aspen of Cowgirls and Indians Resale, for loaning me her incredible and ever-changing examples of what real cowgirls wear;

☆ Karin Cody, who allowed me into her private world at Camp Cody;

☆ Michael Everson, because he helped me untangle my rope countless times; and

☆ Finally, Elsa, the world's best Australian shepherd, who was with me every step of the way for thirteen years.

—Jill Charlotte Stanford

PREFACE

I reckon a girl can be anything she sets her mind to . . .
—Annie Oakley

Not long ago, I was invited to participate in a radio interview for a book I had written, *Wild Women and Tricky Ladies* (Globe Pequot / TwoDot Books, 2010). The book focuses on the wild women of the West, along with trick riders, past and present, who perform daring feats of horsemanship on galloping horses. The stories and illustrations reveal women who are not afraid to take chances, and who look life right square in the eye. They all seem to live by a code of fearlessness, daring, honesty, and courage.

One of the callers that evening lamented the fact that she "had always wanted to be a cowgirl," but, she went on, "I don't live on a ranch and I don't have a horse."

It seems to me that a ranch, a horse, and wide-open spaces are not really necessary to achieve a cowgirl state of mind and to shape your cowgirl attitude.

When you recognize your true inner cowgirl, you will see a world based on the principles that cowgirls live by. You can "brand" yourself with a personal style and a way of conducting yourself, whatever your circumstances. You can obtain a "herd" of family and friends that you can handle with ease. You can rebuild falling-down fences to establish your personal boundaries. You can dress the part authentically, live with items found in a ranch house, and learn the lingo. You *can* be a cowgirl, even if it's just "at heart."

For all of you who wish you had been born on a ranch, had Dale Evans and Roy Rogers as parents and Trigger out in the stable, saddled and bridled and ready to gallop into the sunset, I sincerely hope this book will help you live your own cowgirl life, no matter where you are or what your present circumstances are. You may just discover that you might already be a cowgirl if . . .

Jill Charlotte Stanford

You Might Be a Cowgirl If

. . . if you wear your Victoria's Secret flannel pajamas and a pair of cowboy boots to feed the horses in the morning.

. . . if you have hay in the pockets of all your jackets.

. . . if you have hay in your bra.

. . . if you know all the words to all the Dixie Chicks' songs.

. . . if you've ever swaggered around in real or pretend boots.

1

SADDLE UP! FINDING YOUR INNER COWGIRL

I figure if a girl wants to be a legend she should just go ahead and be one.

—Calamity Jane

Lucille Mulhall, who was known as "America's Greatest Horsewoman and Queen of the Range," caused a sensation and a media frenzy when she appeared at Madison Square Garden in 1905. Some headlines trumpeted FEMALE CONQUEROR OF BEEF AND HORN AND LASSOER IN LINGERIE, while others took a simpler route, calling her a COWBOY GIRL and RANCH QUEEN. Eventually they managed to invent a word that aptly described the lifestyle and talents of a woman who could rope and ride and do ranch work alongside men, and that word was *cowgirl*.

Considered quite shocking according to the late-Victorian customs of the day, these women—clad in leather split skirts, ten-gallon hats, and high-heeled cowboy boots—were competing against the cowboys in bronc riding, steer wrestling, and fancy riding and roping. Better yet, they were winning not only the prize money but the hearts of the fans, who had never seen anything like this before. Genteel they were not; brave and daring they certainly were.

From the beginning, cowgirls captured our imaginations. We gasped at their derring-do. They rode like the wind, tamed the meanest broncs, could do fancy roping, and shoot revolvers and rifles. They never seemed to lose their femininity—even when they landed in the mud, thrown off the top of a "twister." They were good sports and well liked among the cowboy contestants.

Cowgirls like Bertha Kaepernik-Blancett, Goldie Griffith, Mabel Strickland, Bonnie McCarroll, Goldie St. Claire, Ruth Roach, Tad Lucas, Lucille Richards, Lorena Trickey, Fox Hastings, Ollie Osborn, Bonnie Gray, Lulu Parr, Lucille Mulhall, Prairie Rose Henderson, Bea Kirnan, Buckskin Bessie, Florence La Due, Tillie Baldwin, Florence Hughes, Annie Oakley, the aptly named Calamity Jane, Lillian Bergerhoff, May Lillie, and Vera McGinnis were top attractions at rodeos and Wild West shows throughout the United States and Canada. This is just the short list of famous women who were proud to call themselves cowgirls, some of whom traveled to Europe with the popular Wild West shows to show their stuff to large and appreciative crowds that often included royalty.

The vast majority of women who could now be called cowgirls were out on the open ranges and prairies. Spouses of ranchers and cattlemen, some quite alone on the prairies, they rode herd, doctored sick calves, and harnessed the horses that pulled the chuck wagon. They worked side by side with the men in all weather.

Early motion pictures made the cowgirl ideal an icon that has lasted to this day. Many of the early Wild West show and rodeo performers became the first cowgirl movie stars. Two of the most beautiful cowgirls of their day, Florence Hughes Randolph and Mabel Strickland—both of whom began as rodeo performers doing trick riding—were both Metro-Goldwyn-Mayer star attractions.

In the 1930s, Barbara Stanwyck, Joan Crawford, Dorothy Page ("The Singing Cowgirl"), and, the most famous of them all, Dale Evans, were glamorous representatives of a way of life that dazzled young girls in darkened movie theaters throughout the land and, later, on television. I was one of those bedazzled girls. Every Saturday matinee at the Princess Theatre in Edmonds, Washington, you could find me enraptured by Dale Evans. I thought Roy was cute, and Trigger was a beautiful horse, but I wanted to *be* Dale Evans. I wanted to be a cowgirl.

What about those of us who don't live on a ranch, have a horse, couldn't identify a tractor at fifty paces, and go into our offices in suits and high heels—but still yearn to be a cowgirl? I like to think of the secret inner selves of these women as their cowgirl alter egos. I imagine the "biker chick" with a rose tattoo

A cowgirl looks life square in the eye. She will always win a stare-down contest.

on her thigh, black leather miniskirt, studded leather jacket, wild hair, thigh-high boots, mirrored wraparound sunglasses, big motorcycle imagined by Pat Brady and drawn by Don Wimmer as the alter ego for stay-at-home mom, Rose, in the popular syndicated cartoon strip, *Rose Is Rose*. When faced with life's difficulties, Rose climbs on her bike (in her mind) and roars off for some excitement, returning a happier and better person. She feels stronger and in control of the situation again.

> *You might be a cowgirl if . . . someone is ranting at you during a PTA meeting, in line at the grocery store, or at the office, and they don't know that you have quietly cocked your imaginary .38 Colt revolver and are planning to shoot at the floor around their feet to make them dance.*

We all have dreams as we grow up—perhaps you imagined yourself as a princess or a rock star, complete with a regal and demanding attitude or annoying rock-star fashion. But maybe, like I did, you wanted to be a cowgirl, fashioning stick horses to ride and demanding "grub" for dinner. (Cutting my best—and only—skirt so it would have "fringe" at the bottom did not go over well with my mother.) You might be a cowgirl if you swaggered around in real or pretend boots and acted out tales of heroic proportions, all the while mounted on a beautiful horse unseen by mere mortals (but very real just the same). Since you are reading this book, chances are you might be a cowgirl too.

You might not live on a ranch or own a horse, but you can still have a cowgirl as your alter ego, helping to direct your life in all its aspects.

I think that the cowgirl in all of us will find a way to come out when we are ready. Mary Rivers, a trick rider, trainer of trick horses and riders, and mother to trick riders and six-gun shooters, says this:

> *You have to be tough to be a cowgirl. It isn't an easy life, but I,*
> *for one, can tell you that I would not have chosen any other life*
> *if I could have. My whole life has been one great experience after*
> *another. The cowgirl way is a rocky road, but the memories are better*
> *than anyone could imagine. Us old cowgirls have interesting and*
> *entertaining stories. My life has been hard but very, very full. It's*
> *the cowgirl way. It takes a strong woman to be a cowgirl.*

Cowgirl Nancy Becker, a master glass artist and teacher of intuitive skills in central Oregon, knew from the age of four that her life "would be woven with horses." As a young girl, she couldn't understand it when, in spite of her practically saint-like behavior, a much-desired horse or pony didn't materialize on her birthday or under the Christmas tree. Even at the age of four, she identified herself as a horsewoman. A tiny four-year-old horsewoman, but a horsewoman nonetheless.

For Nancy, it felt like her heart exploded when she realized her inner self loved horses, and that she *belonged* with them. "I loved horses with every thread of my being, and I knew this at four years old," she says firmly. "I remember this thought from my ever so independent four-year-old self."

This determined little girl eventually grew up and acquired horses of her own, and as an adult, Nancy's horses have become her teachers—they help her identify a philosophy of life that she calls "Cowgirl True." To her, this means that you are naturally consistent and true to your inner self.

A cowgirl will shoot straight—honesty is a cowgirls trademark. She never cheats . . . on anything.

There are times in our lives when we need to put ourselves first in line. We are set free from uncertainty, doubts, and a great deal of struggle when we finally give in and listen to our inner self. We may find this inner self early or late in our lives, but we will find it, because it is relentless. It's always there, calling us to be true to our own heart, true to our dreams. It's that longing that won't go away—the one that says you want to be a cowgirl, for instance.

Nancy reminds us that "A horse is always a horse, rain will always be wet, and fire will always burn. You, always being the *true* you, means being true to yourself. Don't rein back just to make someone else more comfortable around you."

A COWGIRL'S DICTIONARY

Bandanna: A colorful cloth made of silk or cotton, worn around the neck to protect against winds, rain, and sunburn. Some call it a "glad rag" or a "wild rag," while others call it a neckerchief.

Bedroll: The cowgirl's bed, made up of blankets and quilts wrapped up in a tarp, with hooks or snaps on the sides to hold it all together. Please note that a bedroll is not a down-filled sleeping bag.

Bling: Started as a noun in the 1990s, it is perhaps imitative of light reflecting off jewels. A little sparkle never hurts, and you can find sparkle, or "bling," on boots, hatbands, belts, T-shirts, and jackets.

Branding: Marking cattle or horses with a hot iron that imprints the symbol, or brand, of the cowgirl/owner on the animal's hide.

Broke: This means "trained." A horse that has been given some education is called a broke horse; a green-broke horse is partially trained; a well-broke horse is well trained.

Bronc, or bronco: An unbroken horse, or one that is nervous and wild. Men are very much like broncs in that they have to be handled with extreme care. No sudden moves to startle them; lots of carrots for broncs. (It's up to you to figure out what to do for the nervous cowboy.)

Bunkhouse: A recreation house, or a place to sleep. A cowgirl thinks of her place as her own personal bunkhouse: recreation in the form of chick flicks, the music we like, and a proper bunk to bed down in; add a comfy chair, and this makes a great bunkhouse. The chuck wagon is optional (see "Chuck wagon").

Cattle drive: The movement of a herd of cattle from ranches and grazing lands to the railroad lines for shipment to meatpacking plants farther east.

Chaps (pronounced *shaps*): Leather leggings worn to protect a cowgirl's legs from thorns. We should all have our chaps on to protect ourselves from thorny relationships.

Chuck wagon: An important and essential part of a cow outfit; it carries the groceries, provisions, and other utensils that cowgirls need when working out on the open range. The cowgirl's kitchen is her chuck wagon. It is supplied with provisions to feed cowboys (and cowgirls) when they come in from a hard day's ride. The makings for chili, chocolate chip cookies, cold beer—and whiskey, if it's been a particularly hard day—are good provisions to have on hand. Otherwise, the chuck box holds whatever you desire, and that's probably chocolate.

Clove hitch: A knot used by cowboys to tie a rope or lariat to a post. Have a Boy Scout teach it to you.

Conchos: Silver "buttons" that can be used on a horse's bridle, or as an embellishment to a belt. Usually of Navajo design and in several sizes, this is a "must-have" for any cowgirl.

Corral: An enclosure for penning horses or cattle. Just getting a man into a corral is a hard job. It must be done with stealth. Once they are penned, you can work with them gently until you have gained their trust.

Cow horse: A horse trained to stand still, as if tied, when the reins are down. This is a good thing to teach a man (although a purse works better than reins).

Cutting horse: A ranch horse specially trained to single out (or "cut") a steer or horse from the herd. A good cowgirl can cut a good-looking cowboy from a herd in under eight seconds flat.

Dogies: Orphan or motherless calves or yearlings. Most men are like this—needy.

Eating dirt: What happens when you're thrown from your horse. Into every cowgirl's life comes the moment when she is thrown to the ground during a relationship. She just gets up, dusts herself off, pulls her hat down tighter, and gets right back on!

Fore-footing: To rope an animal by the front feet. Often easier than roping the hind feet, but still difficult. Practice, practice, practice.

Heeling: To rope the hind feet. Hey—any way you can rope 'em is fine.

Hobbles: Restraints that fasten around a horse's front legs below the ankle, to keep the horse from running off while the cowgirl is out of the saddle. Can you envision any other way to use these?

Hog-tie: To tie three of an animal's legs together when it's down; sometimes known as "marriage."

Hot roll: A cowgirl's roll of bedding or blankets. A warm comforter, flannel sheets for winter, Pendleton blankets, and several good goose-down pillows are a must in the bunkhouse.

Jerky: Strips of dried meat that can be stored for long periods of time; handy to keep in your saddlebags if you get a little hungry, because of the protein.

Lariat: A cowgirl's rope. You have to think of your lariat as your secret weapon; that is, never let the cowboy know you have one, and when he's roped, give him plenty of slack.

Mustang: A wild horse; often known as a bachelor.

Outlaw: A horse that no amount of riding or handling will break. Sometimes you run across a cowboy like this, where no amount of gentling or handling will tame him. Turn him back into the remuda. Maybe another cowgirl can do better. Hey, it happens!

Poke: A pouch or bag used by cowboys to carry small personal items.

Pulling leather: Holding on to the saddle while you are riding. When the relationship starts to get rocky, hang on tight!

Quirt: A weighted, short-handled whip made of braided rawhide or leather.

Range: An open area of grassland where cattle and horses graze.

Remuda: A collection of saddle horses. Think of men as a kind of remuda—lots to choose from.

Rodeo: A display of skill in bronco busting and roping that began in the 1870s and remains popular in the West today. The Pendleton Round-Up is the granddaddy of them all. Let 'er buck!

Roundup: A gathering together of all the cattle in a herd, to check or count them. Spring roundup is for branding the young calves. Every gathering of cowboys should be viewed as a roundup where you cull out the bad ones and rope and brand the good ones.

Rustler: A cattle thief. This would be a woman who is not a cowgirl, because a real cowgirl would never rustle another cowgirl's cowboy. *Ever.*

Spurs: Made up of heel band, shank, and rowel, the spur is a tool used to persuade—but not injure—the horse.

Stampede: A blind and wild dash of cattle, caused by fear. To be avoided at all costs.

Tenderfoot: A newcomer to the cowgirl life; also called a "greenhorn."

Wild rags (see "Bandanna"): A large bandanna worn around the neck to keep the sun off or the cold and snow out. A favorite among the buckaroo cowboys and cowgirls.

Wrangler: The cowgirl on a ranch or cattle drive who takes care of the horses.

☆ ☆ ☆

. . . and a Little More Cowgirl Lingo

Above my huckleberry: Too hard for me to do.

All hat and no cattle: Not a real cowgirl/cowboy.

All horns and rattles: Someone who is very angry.

Barkin' at the knot: Wasting your time trying to do something useless.

Doesn't use up all his kindlin' to make a fire: Someone who doesn't waste words on small talk.

Don't go wakin' snakes: Don't make trouble.

He's a featherheaded loco: He's a crazy fool!

I'm busted: I've spent all my money.

You Might Be a Cowgirl If

. . . you always remember that when life bucks you off, you just have to dust yourself off, cowgirl up, and get back in the saddle.

. . . you know who the legendary Nudie was.

. . . you always check to see if there is a horse in a horse trailer going down the road.

. . . you can back a horse trailer into a tight spot.

2

RODEO QUEEN RULES
FOR EVERYDAY LIFE

The buckle don't shine in the dirt!

When I was growing up, I was a member of the Roy Rogers fan club. (Dale Evans didn't have one of her own back then, although you can find several fan sites online today.) "The Queen of the Cowgirls" surely lived by the Roy Rogers Riders Club Rules. I tried hard to follow them then, and I believe we still should try our best to follow them now, even if we are not "little buckaroos" anymore:

Roy Rogers Riders Club Rules

1. Be neat and clean.
2. Be courteous and polite.
3. Always obey your parents.
4. Protect the weak and help them.
5. Be brave and never take chances.
6. Study hard and learn all you can.
7. Be kind to animals and take care of them.
8. Eat all your food and never waste any.
9. Love God and go to Sunday school regularly.
10. Always respect our flag and our country.

Every state of the union has rodeos, and all rodeos have a queen. Many also have a court, or princesses. Early rodeos did not have a panel of judges who chose the queen based on the contestants' abilities and skills as horsewomen. Rather, daughters of prominent ranchers were simply invited to be the queen. Often, it was the cowgirl who garnered the popular vote among her community who became the queen. Sometimes the cowgirl who raised the most money toward paying the expenses of the rodeo won the honor. There are other rules (or standards), which we'll discuss later; these are the ones that future rodeo queens aspire to follow in order to wear the tiara and the title.

One of the earliest rodeos to feature what we now refer to as "a rodeo queen" was the Pendleton Round-Up in Pendleton, Oregon, home of the famous "Let 'er Buck!" slogan. In 1910, Bertha Anger worked in a department store called the People's Warehouse, located in downtown Pendleton. She sold the most tickets to the rodeo and won the title, even though she couldn't even ride a horse! The four runners-up comprised her "court," and this royal entourage traveled in the "Westward Ho!" parade in a buggy. According to Virginia Roberts, president of the Pendleton Round-Up Hall of Fame, "Following Bertha, it appears that all of our other queens have been selected by the rodeo's board of directors. These girls apply, are interviewed, ride, and are ultimately selected by the board of directors."

Having a pretty girl on horseback (or a float or buggy) certainly added some feminine charm to a sport that was mostly grit and raw courage from cowboys and the animals hell-bent on throwing them off into the dirt and the mud of the arena.

Ruth Price remembers that she was riding her horse when a member of the chamber of commerce of her small Oregon town drove up and presented her with a white Stetson hat. "That was what the queen of our rodeo wore, so I guessed it was me," she says, laughing. "I didn't 'try out' for the position, but they knew I was a good horsewoman and would do a good job. I was very thrilled." She pauses for a minute and then adds, "I *did* do a good job, too!"

In my little town of Sisters, Oregon, a Professional Rodeo Cowboys Association (PRCA) rodeo is held every second week in June. Starting in 1940, local "princesses" were chosen by local businessmen. The hopeful girls vied for the crown by selling the most raffle tickets for a steer. Today, the competition is fierce, with categories including horsemanship, speaking ability, and presentation.

Famous personalities were automatically crowned. Mabel Strickland, fearless trick rider (and beautiful to boot), was the queen of the Pendleton Round-Up in 1927, and was referred to as "Queen Mabel" for many years following her reign. MGM movie star Lana Turner was the honorary queen of the 1941 Rooftop Roundup in Estes Park, Colorado. She was named by local cowboys in May when she visited the area for a *Look* magazine travel feature.

Today, hopeful cowgirls start preparing at a young age for the prestigious honor of being named a rodeo queen.

Abigail Petersen, Miss Wapello Pro Rodeo Queen 2010, is from Sperry, Iowa, but the road is her home for now. She and her sister Meishja travel the PRCA rodeo circuit as "The Wild Riders," a trick-riding / EquiStunts duo. Growing up, she was mesmerized by the beautiful ladies who raced around the arena in fringed chaps, satin shirts, and cowboy hats with diamond tiaras around the crown. She recalls, "I suppose it's just like any other pageant in that respect. It's a childhood dream. Other girls watched *Miss America* on television; I was watching the cowgirls with big smiles, colorful outfits, and fast horses."

Her views about being a cowgirl and a rodeo queen are simple:

> *It doesn't take a ranch to make a cowgirl. Real cowgirls are the walking tributes to those that have come before them. They honor our heritage with hard work, courage, and perseverance. They are hospitable and kind, following a code of ethics not many uphold these days. They celebrate beautiful, God-given days, and respect their surroundings. They don't know the word "can't," and won't believe*

anything's "impossible." They don't just dress the part—they live it.
Anyone can buy the outfits, but only cowgirls can tell the stories.

She adds this bit of advice: "Be proud of who you are and what you stand for, even if you are only representing yourself. Whether you are acting as a rodeo queen, or just being you, it's important to present yourself in a way that is true to your beliefs and ideals."

If you ask her what being a rodeo queen means to her, she is quick to tell you, "I wear the title because it represents something I love and live by: rodeo. I am so proud of my American heritage and its unique cowboy culture. When it all comes down to it, the chaps, crown, and buckle are just a bonus; being an ambassador for the Western lifestyle is something that I truly enjoy and love to represent."

Believe me, just being pretty and having a flashy horse does not automatically win you the diamond tiara and the silver belt buckle to wear proudly for the rest of your life. No; you must follow a tight set of rules and regulations. Although they might vary a bit from place to place, the basic standards are:

Rodeo Queen Rules for Everyday Life

HORSEMANSHIP

You must be able to ride your horse. Lead changes, fast gallops, short stops—they are all designed to test your abilities on a horse. This is important, because part of your responsibilities as queen include making many appearances on your horse throughout your reign at rodeos, parades, and other community or civic events. Your composure is watched carefully as you guide your horse through the prescribed patterns. Are you smiling the entire time? Even if your horse balks or stumbles, are you calm and composed in the face of possible disaster?

INTERVIEW

You will be asked questions that will prove whether or not you really know the history of your rodeo and your community, and whether you understand the world in which you live. It's just like going for a job interview, where you are being tested on your skills and abilities. Instead of a horse, you might be controlling a computer with ease, knowledge, and, yes, composure. What about your driving record? Your car, after all, is your steed. Do you have a good driving record? Are you are a safe driver? Calm and composed in traffic? The modern term is "keeping your cool," and that is what judges (as well as prospective employers) look for, not necessarily the skill to perform a certain task to perfection. Things don't always go as planned, and this is where calm, cool composure can win you the crown—or the job.

We are being interviewed every day of our lives, often by total strangers. As a cowgirl, it's up to you to be confident in any situation, whether it is a casual get-together, a job interview, or talking with the checkout cashier at the store. Just remember to look everyone right in the eye and speak up with confidence.

PERSONAL APPEARANCE

As a cowgirl, you will always be neat and clean. Remember rule #1 in the Roy Rogers Riders Club Rules? Your hair is clean, your smile is genuine, and you have checked to make sure there aren't any traces of mud (or worse) on your boots. Your clothes fit and are complimentary to your figure, your coloring, and—this is important, so listen up—the task at hand. In other words, you would not wear a cocktail dress to a PTA meeting, would you?

COMMUNITY INVOLVEMENT

Every woman should be involved in some way with her community, whether it's through her church, a service organization, or her children's school. Perhaps not all at once, but at least one of them. This will help you to know what is going on around you, and to be informed. To get involved is to be involved. That's the cowgirl way.

A cowgirl in Arizona has a suggestion for involvement that is a dandy! She says there are animal rescue groups everywhere that need volunteers. Cats, dogs, bunnies, horses, and ponies . . . the list is long, and you can surely find a place with something warm and furry (possibly feathered) that needs some cowgirl love and care by contacting your local Humane Society. They can put you in touch with all the organizations nearby. You can also Google "Animal Rescue Organizations" and find results for your hometown and state, as well as nationwide. Or, you can write a check to any of the animal rescue groups for much-needed food and supplies for the animals.

It should come as no surprise that there is a mentor for rodeo queens. Jamie Dearing Rauch has put her thirty-five-plus years of experience in the world of rodeo queening into her book, *Rodeo Queen University: Teach the Teachers—A Guide for Rodeo Queen Committees.* Jamie says, "I truly believe that every little girl that has ever ridden a horse has either dreamt of being a rodeo queen or a barrel racer!" Her mission statement is "[t]o provide Rodeo Queen Committees with useful tools, helping them to be successful at their job of educating, directing, mentoring, and utilizing young women whom they elect to represent them as their Rodeo." Jamie believes (and I agree wholeheartedly) that it takes just one positive person to help make a difference in a young person's life.

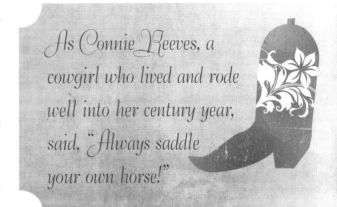

As Connie Reeves, a cowgirl who lived and rode well into her century year, said, "Always saddle your own horse!"

We can take that just a little bit further and encompass all ages. Do you know a senior who is lonely? Perhaps a visit and a plate of cookies would cheer that person up. A friend going through a divorce needs all the support you can muster. A mother of small children would appreciate a cowgirl offering to take the children to the park for a few hours to give the mom some much-needed rest. All of these are positive moves from you, a cowgirl at heart, generous and caring, giving and loving. Not bad attributes to have, wouldn't you agree?

All of Jamie's queens (they affectionately call her "Mama Jams") have something positive to say about their experience. Amanda Emerson is twenty-one, and the daughter of Marilyn and Tracy Oestreich. She attends Central Washington University, majoring in actuarial science with a minor in animal science. She began her queen career in 2007 at a county rodeo, and has worked her way up to the title of Miss Rodeo Washington 2011.

This composed and lovely young woman has this to say about her experience:

> *I am so proud to be the first Native American Miss Rodeo Washington. Being involved with rodeo queening has opened so many doors for me, and has helped me grow into the person I am today. I have the ability to make conversation with anyone I meet; I can make it through the airport in record speed; and I can share how much rodeo means to me and my native heritage. I am proudly from the Colville tribe that is from the Omak, Washington, area. I was born and raised here.*

Mackenzie Carr, Miss Rodeo America 2012, is the daughter of Alan and Barb Carr of Vernonia, Oregon. She grew up on a small farm in a rural timber community an hour from the Oregon coast. Mackenzie was a 2008 graduate and valedictorian of Vernonia High School, as well as a nine-year member of Columbia County Horse 4-H.

Continuing her involvement with the Columbia County Fair and Rodeo, Mackenzie served as one of the 2007 Columbia County Fair and Rodeo princesses and queen in 2008. In 2009, she went on to represent the Northwest Professional Rodeo Association as their Miss NPRA. In July 2010, Mackenzie was in the running for the prestigious title of Miss Rodeo Oregon. In addition to winning that title, she also earned awards for appearance, speech, knowledge, horsemanship, personality, and photogenics. As Miss Rodeo

Oregon 2011, Mackenzie traveled over 30,000 miles throughout Oregon, the United States, and Canada, promoting the great state of Oregon and the Professional Rodeo Cowboys Association. She has this to say about her experience as a rodeo queen:

> *Having the honor to serve as Miss Rodeo Oregon 2011 was truly indescribable. It was by far the best job I could have ever asked for. I had the opportunity to travel across the United States, representing the great state of Oregon and the professional sport of rodeo. As expected, I had an immense amount of fun, but the people I met and the memories I made were simply priceless. The only downfall to holding a position such as this is that it only lasts for 365 days, and then it is passed on to someone new. Would I do it all over again?*

In a heartbeat! I am looking forward to my year as Miss Rodeo America and all the experiences I will have representing our great sport of Rodeo!

Growing up, Mackenzie was surrounded by strong-willed, independent women who helped her to become the person she is today. They taught her to face adversity head-on, to stand her ground, and that showing a little common courtesy would get her far in life. Most important, these women instilled values in her that she embraces in every aspect of her life: dignity, honesty, and humility.

"I view myself as a cowgirl to the core," she says. "I feel I embrace the Western spirit by doing whatever it takes to get the job done. Despite the rodeo queen persona, I am not afraid to get dirty or break a fingernail. First and foremost, I am a cowgirl; being a rodeo queen is just my current job."

If what these cowgirls have to say about their experiences as rodeo queens resonates within you, just remember: Every encounter you have in life is like a rodeo queen interview. Always look your best, be prepared, look the person right in the eye, speak up, know what you are talking about, and say "yes" if they are looking for a volunteer.

That's the cowgirl way.

THE COWGIRL'S GUIDE TO HORSES

If you are considering buying your first horse, there are a few points to consider before you write that check. Of course you have taken riding lessons or you have spent time at a Dude Ranch, so you do know the basics, haven't you? It doesn't matter what breed of horse you choose, what matters is that you and your horse are matched to one another in temperament and size.

Horses are expensive—not only the purchase price but the upkeep. There has been an alarming increase in the cost of hay and grain. Stabling a horse can cost a great deal or very little depending on the accommodations you choose. Then there is the cost of the tack—or equipment—needed to be able to just get on the horse. It doesn't end there. Horses, like people, need new shoes, at the rate of about every six-eight weeks. They get sick. They need a trailer if you want to go anywhere with your horse. The list is endless.

But there is good news. You will not begrudge a single penny spent on your trusted horse. It will be the best money you ever spent. Believe me.

People who do not own a horse, or do not take good care of the horse they own, will be the first ones to tell you how to care for yours.

A handsome horse that is badly behaved will become a lot less attractive in about 15 minutes down the trail.

If the horse dealer insists that the horse is worth twice the price he's asking, you can bet the horse is worth half that amount.

People who think they have nothing more to learn about horses and riding will hit the ground first and the hardest.

The worse a person rides, the faster they will be to blame it all on the horse.

The best way to appreciate how another person rides is to ride their horse.

The richest horse people often look the poorest. Do not be fooled by 'flash.'

I've never met a horse I didn't like. However, I have met quite a few I wouldn't buy.

The smell of a horse when you are standing next to it is the sweetest smell in the world.

Never buy a cheap girth.

You can never have too many hoof picks.

You Might Be a Cowgirl If

. . . you know that courage is being scared to death, but saddling up anyway.

. . . you always remember the Old West saying, "Worry is like a rocking horse—it's something to do that don't get you nowhere."

. . . you don't wait for someone to bring you flowers. You plant your own flower garden so you can have a bouquet every day.

3

ESTABLISHING YOUR BRAND, MENDING YOUR FENCES, AND RIDING HERD ON YOUR DREAMS

When you are at the head of the herd, it's a good idea to look back sometimes to make sure they are still following you.

A cowgirl will register her own personal brand, make sure her fences are tight, acquire some cattle, and ride herd on those cattle. I can hear you saying, "But I don't own any cattle! What herd are you talking about? What fences? A brand?"

Let's start at the beginning. A brand is a permanent mark that is burned onto the hide of cattle to prove ownership. By the time we are ten years old, most of us are "personality branded," which will drive our ambitions and ideals. I was branded as a cowgirl very early in life. Possibly it was the first time I saw Dale Evans on Buttermilk, at the Saturday matinee. As a little girl I would pretend I was riding gallantly on my own (imaginary) horse. I would spend hours "galloping" around our front circular driveway, being chased by bad guys, or on my way to a daring and dangerous rescue of some sort. Two long sticks, held in each hand, were my front legs. I got very good at lead changes with those sticks and could whinny convincingly. My imaginary horse did not have a name, a fact I find odd now, but at the time I simply thought of him as "my horse."

I lived by the code I imagined cowgirls lived by: Always take care of your friends, never leave a cowgirl behind, be honest and true, and, of course, follow the Roy Rogers Riders Club Rules. I was branded for life at that point, even though I didn't have a real horse (not for want of asking, begging, pleading, whining, and cajoling), nor did I live on a ranch, just out in the country. I would realize those goals a little later.

As we grow up, we begin to get away from our childhood dreams and get on with the long journey of making a living, or raising a family, or just trying to make a mark for ourselves during the short time we have on this planet. If you have forgotten what your brand is, just think back on when you were a child and remember your dreams and imaginings. This is the foundation of your life, your "brand." Remember this and you will regain that sense of wonder, optimism, and freedom you felt as a child.

Cowgirl Jan Mendoza has an impressive résumé. She has been a professional musician, performing all over the United States and Europe. She is a professional rodeo trick rider and horse trainer, teaching and coaching would-be trick riders of all ages from around the United States. She has performed at rodeos, fairs, in commercials and other programs on national television, and she has ridden, standing up on her horse Oreo, in the Tournament of Roses Parade. She is the author of two books, *I Was Born to Be* and *I Was Born, Now What?*, and hosts an online motivational program on Your Life Mentor Radio Network. She's currently working on her third book, *Fire Girl,* a memoir about being one of the first female wildland firefighters for the California Department of Forestry. She was branded early on and went on to a life of excitement.

Jan recalls that her determination started early:

> *Every little girl dreams of being something when they grow up. I dreamed of riding my own horse and becoming a cowgirl. I also dreamed of being a professional singer. I remember as a child riding in the backseat of the family car, daydreaming of galloping my very own horse alongside the car as we sped past an open field. Well, when I was nine, I got my own pony, and as my mom and dad drove in the car, I galloped alongside, racing them. I'd had that very same vision, and it came true.*
>
> *I also used to sing into my hairbrush, daydreaming of being on a big stage in front of thousands of people. That very dream happened, many times. I have a habit of taking my daydreams and branding them into my brain. With my dreams forever burned into my mind, I know for a fact that if I think of my dreams often enough, they will eventually come true. When a thought is branded in my head, I have no choice but to take action upon that brand. Little by little my dreams*

become a reality. It's called the power of attraction, and I'm a firm
believer in it. Don't stop dreaming, and brand yourself the person you
want to become. Be a cowgirl, be a professional singer, be anything you
want to be. I did! You can too.

Never one to stand still, even on top of a galloping horse, this dynamic cowgirl has started something she calls "Cowgirl U." She teaches basic horse care, riding, handling, training, tack care, and ranch work—but most important, she teaches cowgirl attitude and etiquette, without which the other skills don't hang together. She says, "I want to take women who are complete beginners—in Western language it's called being a 'tenderfoot'—who always had a passion or a dream to be a cowgirl and horsewoman, and I'll teach 'em everything I know."

Earlier, we explored listening to that voice inside of us that told us we might be a cowgirl. If you've also listened to that voice, and have agreed that yes, you might be a cowgirl, then you were also "branded." You—like Jan and Nancy and countless other cowgirls (including me)—know in your heart of hearts that the cowgirl way is the way for you.

So, you may know what your brand is—you are a cowgirl no matter what anyone says. What will you put that "brand" on? Why, your herd, of course. But just what is your herd composed of? It's a mixed bag. It can be your money, your family, your friends, and your future. It can also be your dreams and your ambitions. Just how big this herd is, is up to you. Make no mistake: It's hard work watching over everything, keeping the whole kit and caboodle in line.

I know a cowgirl who has six horses. They are all beautiful and well trained, but she can't ride them all at the same time, so they languish in her pasture because she is so busy working to earn enough money to pay for their feed, vet bills, and shoeing (not to mention the new tack) she feels she needs for their upkeep. This is a herd—a real one—that is out of control. Not only that, but the fences meant to keep them safe are leaning over, the top rails are all chewed up, and hay-baling twine is used in abundance in an effort to keep the fence from going down completely.

The bigger the herd, the more work for you. Keep it simple so you can take time to smell the sagebrush along the way. Your personal herd—be it great or small—deserves as much attention as the herd of the largest cattle owner in Texas. How you manage it is your own, personal business, but manage it you must. A cowgirl will know where every penny is, where each nickel or dime goes and how she will add to her money "herd" as time goes along. She won't spend randomly, resulting in another untidy herd of "things," milling around and causing dust and confusion that will obliterate the view from your saddle.

If things get out of control, the savvy cowgirl will learn to do several things. First, she will count just how many animals—or how much money—she has. Then she will figure out how much she owes. "Rebuilding her fences" means she will pay off her debts and reestablish control. This might mean you can't buy a new pair of boots every month. Too bad! How many pairs do you really need?

The part of your herd represented by your family and your friends is worthy of constant oversight. Be sure you are up on birthdays, anniversaries, and other events that are meaningful to others. Your small gesture of simply remembering will be appreciated. If you are carrying a grudge, let it go. Ride on ahead with no baggage to weigh you down.

When the West was young and sparsely settled, ranchers had no need of fences or boundaries to contain their horses, cattle, and sheep. The country was so vast, the grasslands so expansive, that they simply turned their herds out to graze with a few cowboys to keep watch over the livestock. In the spring, a roundup was held, with branding and sorting one rancher's livestock from another's, and finally, the long drive to the nearest railhead to ship the fattened stock to market.

When you were young, you had no boundaries either. The world was your playground, full of fascinating surprises—some thrilling, some not so good. Your parents were your herders and kept you out of real trouble. You gradually learned what was dangerous—what was forbidden—and what was considered proper behavior. You were establishing your fence lines, your boundaries.

It might be time to ask yourself how you are doing with your fence lines these days. Remember, your "herds" are your friends and family, your money,

The author, age 11

your relationships—anything at all that affects your life with decisions, right or wrong. How you keep all these things in order, with plenty of room for adjustments, is your job.

Are your fences beginning to sag? Have some fallen down completely? It may be time to put your gloves on, grab the fence-building tools, and ride out there and get them all back up again. Tight fences make good neighbors. They also give the cowgirl peace of mind, knowing she has everything corralled and safe from predators and thieves.

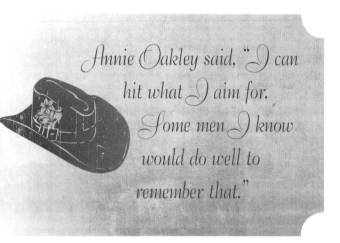

Annie Oakley said, "I can hit what I aim for. Some men I know would do well to remember that."

Be sure to check on that big pasture that holds all your family and friends. Have you returned their telephone calls? Have you remembered a birthday or an anniversary? Have you made time to listen to a friend who might need listening to? Cowgirls are very caring and they pay attention to details. Those details are part of your fence line. Keep it tight.

You might not realize that you are part of the herd you take care of. Perhaps you didn't know that in a horse herd, an alpha mare dictates the direction the family herd travels. The stallion, while flashy and attractive, is not the one to call the shots as to the destination; that's the job of the lead, or alpha, mare.

You are the lead mare, the main herder. You are the one in the saddle, holding the reins, riding herd on and controlling your own, personal herd.

You are the day herder, taking your herd to green grass and fresh water, never rushing them, never spooking them. You are also the night herder, crooning soft songs to keep the herd quiet and bedded down at night. You are always on the alert for varmints and rustlers that want to take your hard-won herd.

Now, about those dreams. Cindy Hooker is a certified coach, human resources leader, and entrepreneur. She has taught English, served in the navy, and worked for Nordstrom department store. One of her most cherished possessions is a pair of forty-plus-year-old cowboy boots given to her by her eighty-year-old uncle. Here is what she has to say about riding herd on your dreams. Listen up.

> *Quit waiting for someone else to make your dreams come true. Why is it so difficult for us girls to ride herd on our dreams? I can't tell you how many times I have talked with a successful gal who rides herd on her work, her family and children, her home, her garden, and yet, she is utterly incapable of riding herd on what makes her heart sing.*
>
> *We all have businesses to run, places to see, art to be created, and books to write. But, if we only had the time, the money, the relationship, or _____ (fill in the blank), then we could do it. Guess what? You have created an obstacle.*

Obstacles you create are terrific distractions from riding herd on our dreams. It's like coming upon a locked gate on the trail you are following. Obstacles provide us with an excuse—an out—a reason why we are not able to get there. "While some folks really do have true obstacles, such as illness, disease, and poverty, most of us seek out and cling to obstacles that hold us back," Cindy says.

Cowgirls are generous. They will gladly give you the western shirt off their back. They are generous with their time, their sympathies, their support, and their recipes.

There is no magic formula for riding herd on your dreams, Cindy cautions. "What a cowgirl needs is clarity, gentle persistence, and compassion. These are the same attributes you use to raise children, train a puppy, or gentle a mustang. You must have a clear vision of where you want to go and what you want done. Then a gentle and persistent movement forward is the next step." Moving backwards serves no purpose, and, just like riding herd, you only go back for the stragglers.

Compassion serves to give you a break. If you make a mistake or have a meltdown along the way, treat yourself with compassion. You might hear a voice in your head saying, "See, I told you—you can't do it." Cindy says, "Simply tell it, 'Yes, I screwed up. But I am still moving forward, whether you like it or not!'"

Follow the trail that moves you forward. "Once you are there," Cindy says, "there is a celebration, there is joy and the contentedness that a cowgirl feels when riding along with a well-mannered herd to its destination."

Here's the bottom line: If you are going to be a cowgirl, and you've decided this is your "brand," then be a cowgirl in every aspect of your life. We only get to ride this range once, and it ought to be a great ride, both for you and for everyone you touch along the way.

You Might Be a Cowgirl If

. . . your pantry has several flavors of barbecue sauce in it.

. . . you think spices are salt, pepper, and red pepper flakes.

. . . you put jalapeños in your meatloaf.

4

MEANWHILE, BACK AT THE RANCH . . .

Home is where the heart is.

Look around your house, apartment, condominium, cabin, or wherever you hang your ten-gallon hat and call home. Does it speak *cowgirl?* Does the place where you spend your private time reflect your inner cowgirl? No?

There are many things you can do to turn your dwelling place into your own private ranch house. You don't need to hang steer heads on the walls or cover all the furniture in animal hides to create an atmosphere that proclaims to all who visit that a cowgirl at heart lives here.

Charlotte inherited from her mother quite a few framed Japanese prints and porcelain vases. They are beautiful and valuable, and Charlotte loves them. "They remind me of my mother," she says, "and they are very calming to look at." But Charlotte's home has a secret. Leave her formal living room with those prints on the walls and Chinese vases on the mantle and walk into her study.

"This," Charlotte proclaims, "is my cowgirl room!"

Here, the walls are covered with framed prints of old-time cowgirls. Over Charlotte's desk, Tillie Baldwin is doing her standing tall in the saddle Hippodrome stand with her arms straight out to the sides and a happy smile on her face. A Pendleton Round-Up queen from the 1930s is gazing lovingly at her saddle horse on another wall. Books about the West and cowgirls fill the bookcase. A miniature saddle, an old bronc stirrup, a lasso, and various other items are on tabletops. A Navajo rug is on the floor.

"My prized possession is this quilt," Charlotte says, lifting an intricate, handmade quilt from a sturdy chair and ottoman. Every fabric square features a Western theme. Running triangles pull it all together, while a hand-embroidered square smack-dab in the middle displays an old-time cowgirl galloping hell-bent for leather. "If the house were burning up, this is what I would carry out," Charlotte says. "It was given to me by a dear friend. It is my cowgirl treasure!"

Author photo

Karin Cody has named her place in the world "Camp Cody," and with good reason. In the juniper and bitter brush of central Oregon, under bright, cobalt-blue skies, Karin has created a Western-themed paradise. Her ranch house has

a "just right" feel to it and is warm and welcoming, beginning with bright red geraniums in galvanized buckets.

Her master bedroom closet features her collection of Old Gringo boots, neatly arranged and displayed on open racks. On another wall are her Western jackets, some with fringe and some with bright silver studs. Her hats are sitting on a high shelf and a variety of Western belts and buckles wait to be threaded through her jeans. Pressed Western shirts are hanging on a bar.

Western memorabilia abounds throughout Camp Cody. A poster for a Wild West show hangs on a living-room wall. A sawed-off six-shooter serves as a handle to open a sliding barn-wood door. A collection of bronze horses, the type given away as prizes at early fairs, sit on a table. Outside, a real tepee is assembled and ready for an overnight guest or a powwow. The overall effect is

Western, cowgirl, and terrific! "I just get carried away," she says with a laugh. "I love everything Western, and especially cowgirl."

Many of the things found in this collector's paradise are not expensive. A bench purchased at a big-box store is covered with a saddle blanket, ready for a cowgirl to sit and pull her boots on or off. It looks like a million bucks. A Pendleton blanket, that icon of the West, serves as her bedspread. Various thrift-store finds of Western-themed creamers that lost their sugar bowls years ago hold wild flowers on the mantelpiece. Mexican Talavera crosses, many of them very rustic, are hanging on one wall, adding a note of color from south of the border.

Like most of the cowgirls I know, Karin enjoys entertaining. Getting together with friends is a great way to catch up on the day's news and share life's triumphs, along with the bumps in the road. Even if you live on the seventeenth floor in the middle of a city, you can create a cowgirl-themed get-together with the foods you choose and the way you present your feast. Believe me, the food does not have to be fancy. It should be simple and nourishing and have the taste of the West. Cowgirls have no idea at all what a "bouquet garni" is, nor do they care to know.

Why not cook up a big pot of chili con carne and make cornbread muffins with butter and honey on them? Or Joan's chile rellenos? The cornbread muffins can be made from a box (I certainly won't tell anyone!).

Author photo

Cowgirls drink wine. They drink beer. They drink iced tea and lemonade. They use Mason jars as drinking glasses instead of fancy and expensive stemware. They shop the shelves at thrift stores. Red-and-white or blue-and-white bandannas (you know the ones) make dandy napkins, or you can use one to line the basket that holds those cornbread muffins. Mix it up. Ranch houses hardly ever had matching dinnerware; they had what survived soapy hands and dish pans.

The sky is the limit, of course, if your budget is big enough to accommodate more-expensive Western flair. A Navajo rug on the floor or hung on the wall as a piece of art is a great focal point for a room. Over the back of a sofa is another good place to display these vividly colored and beautiful handmade works of art. These rugs can be very pricey, but the investment will pay you back over and over again in the pleasure you have looking at them every day.

Perhaps the black-and-white photography of Ansel Adams is your choice? Or, the naughty but nice vintage Vargas pinup girls in their cowgirl poses? Movie posters of old-time Western movies are a good choice as well. If horses are your passion, there are quite a few art posters available in a variety of sizes and subjects. One large colorful print or painting can set the theme for an entire room, or it can be a subtle reminder that a cowgirl at heart lives here.

Pendleton Woolen Mills, in Pendleton, Oregon (home of the famous Pendleton Round-Up—Let 'er Buck!), has been in business for well over a hundred years. The mill began making wool bed blankets and robes for Native Americans in 1895. A study of the color and design preferences of local and Southwest Native Americans resulted in vivid colors and intricate patterns.

These Pendleton blankets were used as basic wearing apparel and as a standard of value for trading and credit among Native Americans. The blankets also became prized for ceremonial use. I can speak from experience: These blankets simply never wear out. I have a prized blanket that I took with me to Camp Tamarack—an all-girls camp located in central Oregon that featured horseback riding, canoeing, and fireside sing-a-longs—more than fifty years ago, and it's still like new. The colors and patterns just speak of the West; used as a bedspread on any style of bedframe, you have an instant touch of the West in your bedroom. Hung on the wall like artwork, it's a perfect complement to any room. There are over a hundred patterns, many of them in different colorways. The "Chief Joseph," named for the famed Nez Perce chief, is still one of the best-selling patterns in Pendleton's line.

Author photo

The small Pendleton "Dopp" bags are made of the same fabric as the blankets, and with the addition of a strap, they make dandy shoulder bags. You can have quite a collection of Pendleton fabrics and patterns without breaking the bank.

Western colors can give one room or your entire house a Western frontier ambiance. Choose colors for Western decorating from nature. Start with earth tones in varying shades. Browns and tans give a warm but understated touch to walls in the living room and kitchen. Using pale blue or sky blue will bring

a peaceful feeling to bathrooms and bedrooms. Painting just the ceiling a sky blue will give you a year-round Western-sky feeling in that room, day or night.

Other colors found in the West are green, orange, red, and deep purple, pink, and yellow. Take color ideas from the earth, grass, sky, sunsets, and animals. Pick medium to light shades of any of these colors from nature and paint the trim a few shades lighter or darker to finish the room. These colors mix well with one another, so if your room is painted brown with straw-colored trim, the rugs, furniture, and any accents can be in several different colors and still blend well.

Wood and leather say Western when it comes to furniture. Brown leather sofas and chairs fit well in almost any Western-theme living room. Other chairs and tables can be made of wood and finished unevenly for a more rustic look.

To make existing wood furniture look more rustic, use a brush and dark stain to add deeper color to the furniture.

Adding brands to leather and wood also gives them a custom cowgirl look. You can find small branding irons online (or see the Resources section). They have all letters and numbers available. Look for an already beaten-up (decorators like to call it "distressed") wood coffee table for very little money

CREATE AN ADOBE MUD LOOK

Purchase a bucket of "mud" or drywall finish and add generous dollops of a southwestern paint color (like peach) to resemble authentic adobe mud. Mix it up and apply by hand for a real southwestern Taos look. Don't be shy! Slap it on. Make a party out of it, and have your cowgirl chums leave their handprints on the wall as a reminder of a fun time.

at thrift stores; with brands burned into it, it looks authentically Old West and like you spent a lot of money (or, better yet, that you stole it from a bunkhouse).

Western-themed fabrics for curtains, pillows, slipcovers, or bedspreads can be found in any fabric store. Don't want cowboys and cattle all over the place? Choose a rough muslin or burlap instead, in shades of brown, beige, or tan.

You can be as creative as you want to be, decorating the entire apartment or house, or just one space to reflect your inner cowgirl. A simple pitcher, found in a thrift store for a quarter and filled with roadside daisies, can be just the perfect small touch.

COME AND GET IT!

Every cowgirl should know a few recipes from the range. All of these tried-and-true recipes are from my first book, *The Cowgirl's Cookbook*. I've given you the Cowgirl's Cornbread recipe to serve with either the Black-Bean Chili or the Chiles Rellenos as your main course, and for dessert, the Kickin' Apple Pie Enchiladas are always a hit. And a few more . . .

If you need more recipes, you can buy the book through my website (www.jillcharlotte.com).

cowgirl's cornbread

1½ cups yellow cornmeal
1 cup whole wheat flour
1 cup unbleached white flour
1 tablespoon baking powder
1 teaspoon baking soda
1 teaspoon salt
2 cups of buttermilk or plain yogurt
½ cup milk
¼ cup maple syrup (or brown sugar or honey)
2 eggs, beaten
¼ cup butter, melted and cooled

Butter a 9x13-inch baking pan or a 2-inch iron skillet.

Sift the dry ingredients into a large bowl. In another bowl, combine all the wet ingredients and stir until mixed.

Fold the wet ingredients into the dry ingredients. Smooth the batter into the pan or skillet and bake at 350 degrees Fahrenheit for 25 to 30 minutes, or until a straw inserted in the center comes out clean.

Cool for at least 10 minutes before cutting into squares.

Makes 12 pieces.

black-bean chili

1 pound of ground beef or beef cut into small chunks
2 tablespoons cooking oil
$\frac{1}{2}$ cup chopped onion
2 28-ounce cans whole tomatoes with juice, crushed
1 tablespoon instant beef bouillon or beef base (1 cube)
$\frac{1}{4}$ teaspoon garlic powder
1 teaspoon cumin
2 15- or 16-ounce cans black beans, rinsed and drained
1 4-ounce can diced green chilies (mild, medium, or hot,
    depending on your taste)

In a heavy skillet, brown the beef and drain. Remove from the pan.

Sauté the onion in the cooking oil.

Add the tomatoes and all the spices. Stir well. Heat to boiling, stirring often.

Add the black beans and chilies.

Add the drained and browned beef.

Reduce the heat to low and simmer, covered, for 30 minutes, stirring occasionally.

Serves 6 to 8 hungry cowgirls.

joan's chiles rellenos

3 7-ounce cans whole green chilies
1 pound Monterey Jack cheese, grated
1 pound cheddar cheese, grated
3 eggs, beaten
3 tablespoons of flour
1 small can evaporated milk
1 15-ounce can tomato sauce

Wash the chilies, remove any seeds, and pat dry.

In a 9x13-inch baking pan, layer half the chilies, then half the cheeses. Repeat the layers, reserving $1/2$ cup cheese as topping.

Beat the eggs, add the flour and milk, and beat until blended.

Pour the egg mixture over the chilies and cheese. The casserole can be refrigerated at this point.

Bake at 350 degrees for 30 minutes. Spread the tomato sauce evenly over the top, sprinkle with the reserved cheese, and bake 15 minutes longer.

Cut into squares to serve.

Serves 6 to 8.

kickin' apple pie enchiladas

2 tablespoons corn starch
2 cups apple juice or apple cider (sweetened)
5 medium tart apples
1 tablespoon lemon juice
1 can chipotle chili pepper in adobo sauce
2 teaspoons butter
¼ cup sugar
1½ teaspoons cinnamon
10 6-inch flour tortillas
additional sugar and cinnamon, as needed

Combine corn starch with an equal amount of water in a small container; stir until dissolved. Heat the apple cider and corn starch to boiling on medium-high heat, stirring constantly. When it begins to thicken, allow to boil for another 30 seconds. Remove from heat, cover, and set aside.

Core, peel, and dice apples to about 5 cups. Place apple cubes in cold water with about 1 tablespoon of lemon juice to prevent them from browning.

Seed and chop the chipotle chili pepper.

In a sauté pan, melt the butter. Drain the apples and add them to the pan. Cook over medium heat until they begin to soften, about 5 to 7 minutes. Then stir in the sugar and cinnamon and $\frac{1}{2}$ teaspoon chipotle pepper (less if you want it mild, more if you like it hot), and about $\frac{1}{2}$ cup of the apple cider sauce. Cook another 3 to 5 minutes. Take off heat and set aside for assembly of enchiladas.

Assemble the enchiladas by placing about $\frac{1}{4}$ cup of the apple cube mixture in the middle of a 6-inch tortilla. Roll up and place side by side in a well-buttered 7x11-inch baking dish, seam side down (8-inch square baking dish will also work, but it will only hold about 8).

Pour remaining apple cider sauce and any remaining apple mixture over the enchiladas. Sprinkle with additional sugar and cinnamon and bake in a 350-degree oven for 25 to 30 minutes, or until the sauce is bubbling and the enchiladas are beginning to brown.

Serve with sharp cheddar cheese and vanilla ice cream.

Serves 4 to 6.

prairie rose's desert rose

1 jigger (4 ounces) tequila
1–2 drops Tabasco Sauce
shaker of salt
wedge of lime

Pour tequila into a small clear highball glass. Gently add Tabasco to the tequila. Watch it as it forms a rose shape in the glass. Lick the V between your thumb and index finger. Sprinkle with salt. Take a bite of lime, lick the salt, and down the hatch with the "rose." Chase with another bite of lime.

Serves 1.

buttermilk honey biscuits

2 cups flour
2 teaspoons baking powder
$1/2$ teaspoon baking soda
1 teaspoon salt
$1/4$ cup shortening
1 cup buttermilk (powdered will do fine)
$1/4$ cup honey

Sift the dry ingredients into a large bowl. Cut the shortening in with a fork until it resembles cornmeal. Add the buttermilk and honey and mix well.

Roll out the dough to a thickness of 1 inch and then cut out rounds using a glass. Place in a lightly greased pan and bake at 350 degrees until golden brown.

Makes 16 biscuits.

the bunk house favorite tuna-egg casserole

2 tablespoons butter
1 cup chopped celery
1 can cream of mushroom soup
½ cup water
1 can tuna, drained
2 teaspoons grated lemon peel (but only if you have it)
4 hard-cooked eggs, sliced
½ cup shredded cheese

Preheat oven to 350 degrees.

Melt the butter in a small skillet. Sauté the celery in the butter until almost tender.

In a small bowl combine the mushroom soup and water. Then add the tuna and lemon peel. Add three of the eggs; save one for the top.

Pour mixture into a one-quart casserole dish and bake for 30 minutes. Garnish the top with the shredded cheese and the last egg slices.

Serves 4.

 You Might Be a Cowgirl If . . .

hens arms

4 tablespoons vegetable oil
2 pounds chicken wings
1 cup honey
½ cup catsup
½ cup cider vinegar
Soy sauce (optional)

Preheat oven to 325 degrees. In a skillet, heat the oil and fry the wings until golden. (Tuck the end part of the wing under the other two parts to "fold them up.") Drain the wings and put them in a Dutch oven or casserole.

Combine honey, catsup, and vinegar (and soy sauce if desired). Pour this over the chicken, cover and bake for 30 minutes.

Makes approximately 18.

steak and beans

For the beans:
2 cups dried pinto beans
1 tablespoon bacon grease
1 clove garlic, minced
1 medium onion, peeled and chopped
1/2 cup tomato sauce
2 teaspoons Worcestershire sauce

Cover the beans with water in a large saucepan and soak for 24 hours. Then add the bacon grease to the soaking water. (This will prevent the beans from boiling over.)

Add the remaining ingredients. Cook at least 8–10 hours over low heat, covered, stirring occasionally. Do not salt while cooking.

For the steak:
1 round steak, about 2 pounds
¼ cup flour
4 tablespoons of vegetable oil
Salt and pepper, to taste
1 cup whole milk

Tenderize the meat by crisscrossing it with a sharp knife, then pounding it with the side of a heavy plate or lid. Roll the tenderized meat in half the flour.

Fry the meat in hot oil for 5 minutes per side. Remove from pan, place it on a platter, and keep it warm in the oven.

Sprinkle remaining flour in the drippings, scraping for the browned bits. Pour in the milk and stir until thickened. Add salt and pepper to taste.

Serves 4 to 6.

tamarack baked carrots

24 large carrots, peeled and sliced
½ cup butter
½ cup brown sugar, packed
½ teaspoon baking powder
2 eggs, beaten
1 cup evaporated milk
Salt and pepper to taste
¼ cup bread crumbs

Boil the carrots until they are "al dente" or nearly done. Drain.

Preheat oven to 350 degrees. Add the butter to the cooked carrots, then mash them. Stir in the remaining ingredients except the bread crumbs and mix well.

Pour carrots into a greased casserole dish. Sprinkle on the bread crumbs and bake for 30 minutes or until the bread crumbs are browned.

Serves 8 (but doubles well to serve 16).

kentucky corn pudding

3 tablespoons butter, room temperature
2 tablespoons sugar
2 tablespoons flour
1 teaspoon salt
3 eggs
2 cups fresh, frozen, or canned (drained) corn kernels, coarsely chopped
1$\frac{1}{2}$ cups half-and-half or heavy cream

Preheat the oven to 350 degrees. In a buttered 1$\frac{1}{2}$ quart casserole dish, mix the butter, sugar, flour, and salt. Beat in the eggs, and stir in the corn and cream.

Bake for 45 minutes until slightly puffed and brown.

Serves 6.

high desert potato and bacon soup

3 large potatoes, peeled and cubed
1 medium onion, peeled and cubed
1 quart water
Salt and pepper to taste
5 strips bacon
1$\frac{1}{2}$ cups bread crumbs from stale bread
$\frac{1}{2}$ cup cream (evaporated milk will do)

Cook the potatoes and onion in water until soft. "Mash" them a little bit to release more flavor, but do not drain. Add salt and pepper to taste.

Cut the bacon into small pieces and fry until crisp and brown. Remove the bacon from the fat to drain. Add the bread crumbs to the fat and stir and toast until brown.

Add the cooked bacon and browned bread crumbs to the potato and onion soup and reheat, adding more seasonings if you wish. Stir in the cream or milk.

Serves 6.

fruity salsa

2 kiwi, peeled and chopped
1 cup any melon, chopped
1/2 cup fresh pineapple, chopped
3 or 4 tablespoons red onion, finely chopped
2 tablespoons lime juice
1/2 jalapeño pepper (or more if you like it hot), chopped fine
1/4 teaspoon salt
1 1/2 tablespoons chopped cilantro
1 tablespoon olive oil
Pepper to taste

In a medium bowl, combine all ingredients. Adjust flavors to taste. Cover and refrigerate for 3 hours or overnight. You can substitute any kind of tropical fruit—it all works.

Makes about 2 cups.

mustang chocolate cake

1$\frac{1}{2}$ cups flour
3 tablespoons dark cocoa
1 teaspoon baking soda
1 cup sugar
$\frac{1}{2}$ teaspoon salt
5 tablespoons cooking oil
1 tablespoon vinegar
1 teaspoon vanilla
1 cup cold water

Preheat oven to 350 degrees. Sift the flour, cocoa, baking soda, sugar, and salt into a greased 9x9-inch square cake pan.

Using the end of a wooden spoon, or your index finger, make three holes in the dry mixture. Into one, pour the cooking oil; into the second, the vinegar; into the third, the vanilla. Pour the cold water slowly over the whole thing. Then beat it with a fork until it's almost smooth and you can no longer see the dry ingredients. Be sure to get into the corners.

Bake for 30 minutes. Serve straight from the pan.

Makes about 12 squares.

You Might Be a Cowgirl If . . .

texas two-step blackberry dumplings

Step One:
2 pints fresh blackberries, washed
3/4 cup water
1 cup sugar
1 1/2 tablespoons butter, softened

Combine all the ingredients in a large saucepan and simmer while preparing the dough, below.

Step Two:
2 cups flour
3 tablespoons sugar
1/2 teaspoon salt
3 1/2 tablespoons baking powder
1 egg
3/4 cup milk

Sift the flour, sugar, salt, and baking powder into a mixing bowl. Add the egg and mix well. Add the milk to make a stiff batter.

Bring the berry mixture back to a boil. Drop the dumpling batter, a large spoonful at a time, into the boiling mixture. Do not crowd the dumplings—be sure they have room to expand as they cook.

Cover and cook for 20 minutes. Lift out with a slotted spoon.

These dumplings are good hot with ice cream or cold for breakfast. If you don't have blackberries, you can use Marion berries, raspberries, blueberries, or ripe peaches.

Makes about 8 dumplings.

You Might Be a Cowgirl If

. . . your idea of jewelry is anything silver and/or turquoise.

. . . when a friend asks, "Are these jeans too tight?," you say, "Honey, yes, they are." Then you go shopping with her for a new pair.

. . . you own at least one item of apparel that has fringe on it.

I SEE BY YOUR OUTFIT
THAT YOU ARE A COWGIRL

I ain't afraid to shoot good, and
I ain't afraid to look good neither.

—Lulu Parr

Indulge me for a moment while I tell you that my first pair of cowgirl boots was made by Acme. They were the "Pee-Wee" style—that is, they were a "short" boot. They were black with white-and-red inlays and overlays. I wore them to Camp Tamarack a girls' riding camp in 1953, where I rode around all day under bright blue Western skies and tall, fragrant ponderosa pines. I loved those boots and wish I still had them. Heck, I wish I were back at that camp, too!

A lot of what we think of when we picture what it means to "dress cowgirl" comes from the fashions of the Wild West shows and rodeos of the late 1800s, where women performed and often competed against men. Costume choices for cowgirls were limited, as they were dictated by the morals and strict post-Victorian fashions of the day. Early rodeo riders and stuntwomen chose to wear gymnastic bloomers when they rode on rough stock, or they wore jodhpurs, which are full-length trousers that flare at the hip and have reinforced patches on the inside of the knee. A silk shirt and bandanna, a large Western hat, and tall English-style boots completed their look, and off they went—quite literally. When they were thrown from their horses, they discovered that the bloomers presented a real life-threatening danger, as the bloomer legs would hang up on the saddle horn. One competitor lost her bloomers completely, along with the contest. Tilly Baldwin, a noted trick rider, kept the bloomers as her personal fashion statement. She had been a gymnast in her native Sweden, and learned to fasten the bottoms of the bloomer legs with elastic to avoid those nasty hang-ups.

Early cowgirls loved their boots, and cowgirls today love them just as much. Cowgirl Cassie Hoffober wrote, "How many pairs of cowboy boots can you own before they plan an intervention? Just wondering . . . no particular reason . . . Note to self: Need more boot shelf space."

Leather split skirts began to make their appearance in the late 1800s. Embellished with fringe and silver buttons, the weight of the cowhide helped the women stay aboard and didn't rip or hang up on the saddle horn. The skirts were considered almost decent, and they were safer because they allowed cowgirls to ride "astride"—that is, with one leg on either side of the horse, rather than the formal sidesaddle mode of riding for ladies—a fashion that was becoming acceptable—almost. The chaps women and men wear today serve the same purpose as those early split skirts. They not only protect the riders' legs from brush and thorns and cattle horns, but the weight of the leather also helps to keep the rider in place on the saddle.

The early women trick riders and Wild West performers were daring, it's true, but they also had a sense of style. They loved their fancy silk shirts and often sewed them themselves, in bright colors. The silk bandannas they tied around their necks were also brightly colored. Their hats got larger and larger. Stetson made a special hat for Fox Hastings, designed according to her personal specifications. It featured a tall crown and a wide brim. You can easily pick her out in a photograph of a crowd of cowgirls simply by looking for that hat. Leather gloves protected their hands and were quite stylish. The fringed and beaded gauntlets, with wide wristbands, were brightly beaded, as were the belts they wore over their leather skirts.

Tall boots were a must. High, undershot heels helped the girls wedge their feet into the stirrups on a galloping or bucking horse. While the foot part was utilitarian, the top—or shaft—was a place to let loose their cowgirl style. Embroidered flowers, vines, tooled roses, playing cards as an inlay (beneath the outer leather), or overlays of their initials were popular. Their choice of designs was dictated by how much they could spend.

Gradually, the fashions of the early riders began to change. By the 1940s and '50s, dude ranches were becoming very popular, as men and women rediscovered the "Wild West." Dressing the part was fun, but it had to be practical as well.

The popular gabardine fabric, a sturdy, tightly woven material of cotton, wool, or rayon twill, was a perfect choice for stylish Western apparel for both men and women. Many fashionable department stores had special sections devoted especially to dude ranch wear.

A travelogue film called *Dude Ranch Fashions*, produced in 1948, gives us an insider's look at what women were wearing in the Wild West when they visited the Flying L Ranch for a holiday. The prop plane lands, and as four women come down the gangway, they are greeted by cowboys on horseback. The next shot features the would-be cowgirls sitting on the top rail of the corral, watching calf roping. All of them are attired in Western-themed skirts and blouses, some with fringe embellishment. At the square dance that evening, calico and cotton dresses with scoop necks and tiered skirts whirl gaily as the cowboys do-si-do with them around the dance floor. They ride to a campfire cookout in "frontier pants," boots, and Western shirts. (See Resources section for more information about viewing excerpts from this travelogue online.)

Boots were changing their look too. No longer was the tall boot with the high, undershot heel meant only for the rodeo rider and working cowboy; cowgirl boots were becoming a fashion statement as well as riding wear. One example is the Acme Boot Company, founded in 1929. One of the founders and owners went to Texas on business and saw a pair of Western boots that cost sixty-five dollars—well beyond the reach of the average shoe buyer at the time. He bought a pair of boots to see how they were made, carefully studying them and noting every detail of their construction. Based on his inspection, Acme decided they could produce the same boots on an assembly line, allowing them to sell the boots for a better price. In the 1940s, Acme Boots became the world's largest producer of cowboy boots, and remained so until the mid-1980s.

Today, cowgirl boots are back in fashion (many say they never went out), and the sky is the limit! Short or tall, made of serviceable or exotic skins and leathers, tooled by hand or machine, you are limited only by your imagination and possibly your pocketbook. Me? I prefer a well-worn pair of comfortable boots, scuffed and dusty, showing miles of trails ridden. Who is to know whether they've ever seen a stirrup? The point is, if you do buy a new pair, scuff them up! "Brand-new" is not a cowgirl look. (New boots can be uncomfortable. To soften them, fill them with hot water, empty the water out, put them on with socks, and wear 'em till they're dry. They will fit to your feet. Then use Justin Boots leather conditioner or saddle soap to keep them pliable.)

Hats were also undergoing changes. It is not clear when what we call "the cowboy hat" began to be named as such. Westerners originally had no standard headwear. The working cowboy wore wide-brimmed, high-crowned hats long before the invention of the modern design. Wide brims for shade and a high crown, along with a "stampede string" worn under the chin to keep it from flying off, was a style that emerged out of necessity. As one cowboy put it, "The cowboy hat kept the sun out of your eyes and off your neck. It was an umbrella. It gave you a bucket [the crown] to water your horse and a cup to water yourself. It made a hell of a fan, which you need sometimes for a fire, but more often to shunt cows this direction or that."

Style today varies from short crowns to tall, wide brims to narrow. Cowboy hats are still made of wool felt (for winter), in black, brown, beige, gray, or "silver

WEARING YOUR HAT

There are only four rules for a cowgirl when wearing a cowgirl hat:

1. Never, ever put the hat on the back of your head. This will immediately mark you as a dude. Be sure your hat is your correct size. An experienced salesperson in a Western apparel store will help you to determine this. Place the hat first on your forehead and then push it firmly down on your head. It should be level, not tipped back.

2. Wear a Panama straw in the summer because it's cooler than a felt hat, and a felt hat in the winter because it's warmer.

3. Never store your hat on its brim. Either turn it upside down or use an empty five-pound coffee can for a hat stand. The hat will retain its shape this way.

4. And lastly, if I hear that you went out and bought a pink straw, I will personally hunt you down, snatch it from your head, and stomp on it.

Author photo

belly," and straw (for summer), known as the Panama.

A good pair of Wranglers, well washed and worn (remember that rule about looking new?), a Western shirt (you can really go crazy here because there are so many choices—just make sure the shirts have the traditional "pearl snap" fastenings), and a fringed jacket will round out your wardrobe. Let's take these items of apparel one at a time.

Your jeans should reflect that you are, indeed, a cowgirl. I know there are other brands out there, many of them sporting embellishments and two-inch zippers, but these are not what the true cowgirl wears. Wranglers have a secret: There is no double seam on the inside of the leg because that double seam will cause rubbing when you're in the saddle. Go to a rodeo and look at what the real cowboys and cowgirls are wearing. Yep—Wranglers. Wash the living daylights out of them, make sure they fit snug but not tight, and be sure they are long enough to "stack"—that is, when you are standing in your boots, there should be two or three folds of fabric down by your feet. Why? Because when you get on a horse, the pants will hike up, creating a high-water look that is also death to a would-be cowgirl.

Having a black pair for "dress-up" is also a good idea.

A good leather jacket, with fringe, is your best Western accessory. Look for brands like Double D Ranch, Scully, and Pioneer Wear. They have all endeavored to make jackets both short and long that reflect the true Western heritage. Look on eBay for great finds, and if it shows a little wear, so much the better! Consignment stores often have these jackets, and at less than half the original price (see the Resources section). Wear this fabulous jacket with a skirt, your jeans, a dress, dress pants and heels, or any way you want. A leather jacket is a fashion statement (Ralph Lauren knows this too), and the feeling of that fringe dancing on your body is really wonderful.

What about jewelry, and what has been termed "bling"? Cowgirls traditionally wear silver in the form of concho earrings, silver hoop earrings, silver beads, necklaces, and cuff bracelets, and very often

Author photos

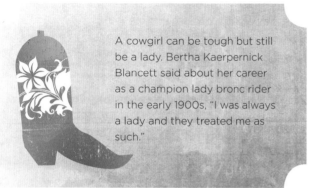

A cowgirl can be tough but still be a lady. Bertha Kaerpernick Blancett said about her career as a champion lady bronc rider in the early 1900s, "I was always a lady and they treated me as such."

these items are embellished with turquoise. "Bling" is anything with rhinestones or other sparkly things on it. I think a little bling is all right, but don't go overboard!

Your belt should be tooled leather with a silver buckle, tip, and keeper. A trophy buckle can only be worn if you have won it fair and square. If you are wearing a simple little black dress or a swirly prairie skirt, a Navajo silver concho belt is a true addition, as well as a valuable keepsake to pass down through the generations.

Women of all ages and from all walks of life who live and love the Western lifestyle strive to preserve and promote it. From students to attorneys, flight attendants to models, horse trainers to ranchers—they all share a common love for all things Western, both old and new. These women don't just wear the costume; they live the life. A modern term for them is *cow-diva*.

The cow-diva's fashion philosophy is all about embracing her true cowgirl soul and finding what works for her personally. It's all about individuality. Their only hard-and-fast fashion rule is: Never leave the house without the three most important fashion accessories—a smile, a kind word, and a positive attitude. Those things can spruce up just about anything you're wearing. You can go all out with fringe and turquoise, a ten-gallon hat, fancy boots, and well-fitted jeans, or you can simply make a statement by wearing a skirt or sundress with your scuffed cowboy boots. The choices are many; the style part is up to you.

ON THE ROAD AGAIN: A COWGIRL PLAYLIST

I asked some of my cowgirl friends to tell me their favorite songs—the ones they listen to while speeding down the back roads in their trucks, kicking up dust. Some of the answers were surprising and some were predictable, but all of them are wonderful. What's on your playlist?

Whispering Pines
Johnny Horton

How 'Bout Them Cowgirls
George Strait

Barrel-Racing Angel
Ian Tyson

Whatever It *Is*
Zac Brown Band

Thrift Store Cowgirl
Red Meat

Save a Horse, Ride a Cowboy
Jan Mendoza

My Rifle, My Pony and Me"
(from *Rio Lobo*)
Dean Martin and Ricky Nelson

Strawberry Roan
Joan Triplett

Loves a Rodeo
Wooden Eye

Girls and Horses
Templeton Thompson

Like a Prayer
Madonna

The Trail Less Traveled
Mary Ann Kennedy

The Cowgirl Song
Patsy Montana

Cowgirl Pride
K. D. Lang

Keep 'Er Steady, Cowgirl
Chuck Pyle

Even Cowgirls Get the Blues
Emmylou Harris

Happy Trails
Roy Rogers and Dale Evans

You Might Be a Cowgirl If

. . . the only thing that makes you weak in the knees is a newborn foal, puppy, or kitten.

. . . you are not afraid of firearms. Hell, you own a firearm.

. . . you can drive a straight-shift 1972 Ford pickup truck.

------- **6** -------

THE COWGIRL WAY

When it comes to life's adventures,
never pull back on the reins.

Countless women throughout history have exemplified the cowgirl way through their actions, either on or off a ranch, and some in the canyons of big cities. Some, like the early rodeo riders and trick riders, gained notoriety immediately, while others earned fame long after they were gone from the Western lands they loved. There are women today who define the cowgirl's determination to get it done, whatever the task at hand. These women, each in her own way, achieved their goals through exactly what we have been talking about—tapping into their inner cowgirl.

Here are four women's stories that I hope will help guide you to achieve your goals. All of them have courage and grit as well as a healthy dose of humor.

Mary McConnell Laird: Into the West

Mary McConnell Laird was born in 1900 in Hollyoak, Colorado. Her family moved east to Kansas City, Missouri, when she was very young, but then looked west again, to Cokeville, Wyoming. She remembered traveling west in a covered wagon, as a young girl of eight, carrying chickens in a box on the back of the wagon. When a hen would cackle they would stop and gather the egg. The family's trail diet consisted mostly of eggs, beans, and small wildlife such as rabbits. The kids had the job of gathering cow chips to cook with. She said the food tasted just like it smelled when it burned over the fire.

Mary met her first husband, Elmer McConnell (called Mac), while they were both working on neighboring ranches. They married and began homesteading east of Gillette, Wyoming. Their small acreage would not sustain enough livestock to make a living, so Mary took a sheepherding job and Mac worked as the camp tender for several of the sheep ranches in the area, delivering groceries, wood, and other staples to the herders once a week.

The sheep wagons that herders lived in were functional, although certainly not comfortable by any means. They were outfitted like primitive RVs. The stove was very small and would not hold a fire throughout the night. During the cold winter nights Mary would have to take her potatoes, onions, and canned goods to bed with her to keep them from freezing. She read every book she could get her hands on, as that was her only entertainment. Her companions consisted of two working sheepdogs and one saddle horse that was also broke to pull the wagon from one camp to another.

Her granddaughter Mary Roberts says, "She took some time off herding when my dad [Earl McConnell] was born, but returned to sheepherding the summer he was two years old, carrying him on the front of her saddle. I remember asking her what she did when she got sick, and she said, 'Sheepherders don't get sick.' The only person they were ever in contact with was the camp tender or the occasional cowboy drifting through the country who would stop by a sheep camp for a meal. She did have a rifle and two good sheepdogs for protection, and only on one occasion did she feel insecure with the visitor."

The McConnells saved up their wages, bought some land adjoining their homestead, and started raising cattle. They were able to make a living on that land until the Great Depression of the 1930s. At that time, land was selling for two dollars an acre, but they didn't have enough money to buy any more land. They had to leave the homestead, and took jobs driving oil trucks to build new roads in the southern part of Wyoming. They continued living in the sheep wagon, camping outside of whatever town they were working near. Granddaughter Mary says, "My dad would hunt rabbits or go fishing throughout the day for food. He could trade the fish for other food staples, mostly beans, at the grocery stores."

The family eventually returned to the homestead and started ranching again. Mary was happy to be home because she could raise a garden, and, because they were back in the cattle business, they had meat on the table once again.

Not everything went well following their homecoming. The difficulties of the prior years had made a mark on Mac, eventually ending in divorce between Mary and Mac. Mary later married her second husband, Alan Laird, but sadly, he only lived for nine months following the marriage. He died of a heart condition during a fierce snowstorm, leaving Mary and her young son to fend for themselves. Mother and son continued ranching, and, with much hard work, they expanded the operation. Granddaughter Mary Roberts recalls, "I believe Grandma had only a third-grade education, and Dad had to quit high school during his junior year due to illness. He never returned. This never hindered either of them in the business world."

Mary McConnell Roberts: Carrying on the Tradition

The Big Sag Ranch—long and complicated with arroyos, gullies, flat land, mesas, and meadows—is located in central Montana. In ranchers' terms, "It runs a lot of cows," and keeping it going is a year-round job.

Mary McConnell Roberts runs the operation almost single-handedly with Frank, her husband of nearly forty years. Mary, granddaughter of Mary McConnell Laird, was born into this life, and she loves it.

"I was born when Grandma was fifty-two years old," she says. "It wasn't long before I was her constant companion." Her early years were spent on the original homestead, where she learned at an early age how to milk cows by hand, work cattle on horseback, drive a feed vehicle, and feed the chickens and hogs.

Mary began first grade in a country school that had only five students. She rode her pony to school, a three-mile ride one way, until the winter weather set in. "I looked forward to that ride much more than the schooling," Mary recalls. "We never had indoor plumbing, electricity, or a telephone, either at home or at school."

By the time she was in third grade, her father Earl began trading real estate. That meant buying and selling ranches, so the family made several moves. They owned two Wyoming ranches, including the original homestead, which had grown much larger by then because they had bought neighboring ranches when they came up for sale. The other ranch was near Cody, Wyoming. Her family owned the Gillette ranch for sixty years, and the Cody ranch for five.

Operating two ranches that were so far apart was hard on the entire family, so both were eventually sold, and the family moved to their first Montana ranch. It was here that Mary met her husband Frank, who was working as a ranch hand on a neighboring property at the time. Frank was a true rancher at heart, and soon took over many of the tasks at Mary's family's ranch.

"I always loved the land and the home where I was living at the time, and hated each move. But soon I grew to love the new ranch more than the one we had left behind," Mary remembers. "I must stress that money was always very short, and it was hard work all the time. Grandma would say, 'We're just gonna have to tighten our belts,' but my thinking was, my belt is already in the last hole!"

Every ranch and location had its own challenges as well as its good points. Mary, her husband, and children are currently ranching in central Montana, where they have a lot of big winds and late-spring storms that make calving, more often than not, very challenging. "But," Mary says, smiling, "all in all, this is the best ranch we have ever owned."

Mary's mother, Mary Joyce Roberts, was a top hand from the kitchen to the corral, and sadly passed away when Mary was still in high school. Her father and her grandmother Mary passed away eight months apart from one another. "My grandmother was just five months away from being a hundred years old. I lived with Grandma until I got married, and then she moved in with Frank and me until her passing."

Mary states firmly,

I wouldn't trade this lifestyle for any other. The good, really good,
days doing what you love outweigh the rough ones many times over.
My favorite days are riding a good horse to move cattle in beautiful,

unspoiled country. I take pride in this ranch, as I always remember the work my ancestors, as well as my husband and I, have put into it to make it what it is today.

I am getting to an age where many people would be considering retirement, but for me, I'm never as happy anywhere as I am on the ranch, doing the daily work—taking care of the animals and land.

The talented photographer for this book, Robin L. Corey, is a close friend of Mary Roberts. Robin has had the opportunity—some would say the gift—of riding with Mary for roundups and branding on the Big Sag Ranch. Robin knows her friend Mary very well.

"'Cowgirl' is a broad term that blankets many people with a common thread, and that thread is their spirit," Robin explains.

A third-generation rancher, Mary knows her livestock as well as she knows herself. She has seen everything from the saddle, in the dust, in a snowstorm, and with the wind in her face. She is defined equally by her work and her spirit—her ethics, tenacity, and her love of the lifestyle. There are no shortcuts to doing a job right, and doing it right the first time. Land and cattle come first in a house that is steward to the outfit.

"All of life revolves around the workday," Robin says. "I have never seen Mary anything but grateful for that, no matter how hard the work is, or what is involved."

Robin has known Mary for twenty-five years, and while their friendship is a strong sisterhood, it is the importance of hard work that Mary has most impressed upon Robin. It's not only the right thing to work hard, but it's also the sense of accomplishment you feel when you start to come toward the tail end of life, and the trail starts narrowing. To look back and know that your hard physical labor paid off and that you contributed to a legacy is better than any gold watch out there.

"Mary's grandmother, Mary Laird, started it all in a sheep wagon. Mary appreciates the hardships her grandmother went through in the early days, and while times may have made the job better in many ways, it still hasn't made it easy. There will always be many jobs on a ranch that will never be replaced by technology, a machine, or office management. Mary has seen her fair share of just about everything life has to offer or dish out. She is a cowgirl in that her sense of adventure never wanes, her pride keeps her motivated, and her guts keep her in the game. She is a leather-and-lace rancher, a wife, a mother, and a grandmother. She is the heartbeat of their home and business," Robin says. Then she adds, "Lucky for me, she is also my friend."

Patti Johnson: Flying High and Shooting Straight

Not many women can be an expert horsewoman in the morning and then pilot a jet airplane in the afternoon—expertly.

Patti Johnson can.

A big influence in Patti's life was her father, Samuel S. "Sam" Johnson, a businessman, legislator, and philanthropist in the state of Oregon. He owned sawmills and large tracks of timberland in central Oregon, where Patti and her

Patti Johnson on Bucky Buckaroo
Catherine Denton photographer/Blink of an eye foto

sister Betsy spent their summers, much of their time spent on horseback. Sam also served seven terms in the Oregon House of Representatives.

Patti says of her dad, "Our father, Sam, wanted my sister Betsy and me to experience 'everything,' and not to be afraid of things that many women feared. When we were growing up, we started to learn to shoot at ages nine and eleven. We handled snakes (nonpoisonous, of course), ran the mousetrap line, fished, were expected to kill any indoor spiders (no matter how large they were), drove the tractors, as well as cars and trucks with manual transmissions, rode horses, played the piano, and soloed in an airplane. Bowling and golf didn't enter into the equation. I really don't think that he was surprised when Betsy and I both decided to become professional pilots. He was a remarkable and amazing man."

Patti found school challenging, first attending a Catholic boarding school in California and later finishing high school in Portland. After graduating, she went to nursing school and worked as an RN. Flying and aircraft mechanics school took up her spare time. She eventually moved to Texas where she taught aerobatics, later becoming a member of the US Aerobatics Team. She won one gold, three silver, and two bronze medals, and was named the US Women's National Aerobatic Champion. The medals were won on the world level in 1982.

Patti's inner cowgirl convinced her to move to Steamboat Springs, Colorado, where she bought a forty-six-acre ranch with a barn. Within a month she had a horse; soon there were five.

Patti eventually took her horses with her to Florida, where she continued her air-racing campaign. She was the first woman to win a national championship pylon air race against men in the biplane class, in Reno, 1993. Next, cowboy mounted shooting attracted this energetic cowgirl. "Top Shot" star and cowboy mounted shooting champion Denny Chapman took her under his wing as a student. He says, "Patti's love for adventure is paralleled only by her love of horses. She is an excellent mounted shooting student and is fond of the Old West and its traditions."

Patti says this about her high-flying life: "If I talked to a stranger on the street and told him about my life, he'd think I was some kind of female Walter Mitty, a 'nutcase,' or a liar."

Sally Bishop: A High-Octane Life

Do one thing a day that scares you.
—Sally Bishop

Sally Bishop will be the first to tell you she likes "stepping out of the norms." As a third-generation rodeo and Wild West performer, she can handle a four-horse Roman riding team at speed, can morph into elegant dressage, or hire on as a stuntwoman for films like *Flicka 2,* or roles in television programs like *Into the West, Heartland,* and others. In her spare time she races Ducati bikes. It won't surprise anyone to learn that she stays fit for these strenuous activities as a certified personal trainer.

She calls Calgary, Alberta, Canada, her home base, but she can be found anywhere in North America, as well as Europe, with Sure Shot Productions—a

Sally Bishop
Photograph by "Shooter"

trick-riding team comprised of Sally and her friend and partner, Roz Beaton. Their act combines trick riding with high-octane speed and daring.

Jan Mendoza, a noted trick rider and teacher, has this to say about Sally Bishop: "She is one of the most stunning trick riders I know. She executes her tricks and stunts with such grace and style, it's like watching a prima ballerina dance."

Sally was born into the life of trick riding and Wild West shows. Her grandfather, Tom Bishop, arrived in Canada as a young boy, dreaming of the frontier. A city boy with no skills, he nearly starved while homesteading in a sod dugout hut during his first Canadian winter. When he saw Buffalo Bill's Wild West Show, he knew that was what he wanted to do, so he began to put on Wild West shows at local fairs. His son, Tom Bishop Sr.—along with his beautiful wife, mother of Tom Jr., Sally, and Sarah—continued his father's traditions, and taught his children the ropes—literally. Tom Jr. has taken his own Wild West shows to the next level, one of many ways he preserves pioneer heritage.

Following high school, Sally thought she would like to have a "real job," so she went to college, majored in environmental sciences, and eventually applied to law school. Then she had a revelation.

"I had been accepted to law school and was two weeks away from starting when I realized that performing was in my blood. A lawyer? That wasn't me. I don't regret it. The funny thing was, when I told my parents I was going to law school, they responded with, 'Well that's boring.'"

Was Sally always a daredevil? Big brother Tom Bishop Jr., also a trick rider, peerless roper, and performer says of Sally,

*Growing up, I never thought that what Sally did was daredevil-
ish. For Sally, our sister Sarah, and me, there was church, chores,
and the family Wild West show. Watching Sally today, whether
the stunning grace of her trick riding or her octane-fueled Roman
riding, I realize that one could call her one heck of a daredevil. She
is an athlete and a perfectionist who has worked hard and paid her
dues. There is nothing as rewarding as leaving an audience wanting
more, and that she does!*

Sally is modest about her accomplishments, which demand courage, skill, and daring. She says, "I seem to be really attracted to putting myself in uncomfortable situations—testing my nerves and my will. I certainly have fear, but I seem to feel the most alive when I face it head-on. Yes, I get nervous; yes, I doubt myself; but I do it anyway, and the feeling afterward—especially when it is successful—is exhilarating."

What else would she like to do with her life, besides risk life and limb perched atop a galloping horse in front of a cheering audience? She smiles and says, "If I could do anything else, I would want to be a triple threat on Broadway! I could see myself onstage doing a mean tap dance, or playing Roxy in Chicago. I guess I really am a performer to the core . . ."

What does being a cowgirl—albeit, a cowgirl who is upside down or standing up on four galloping horses—mean to this beautiful and talented performer? She says, "I think *cowgirl* is a state of mind. I think I have proved you can be from anywhere and be a cowgirl. I grew up in southern Ontario,

Canada! Not exactly cowboy country. My dad taught us to be tough and self-sufficient, and how to go out and make your own way in this world. You work hard and you are grateful for what you have."

And then she adds, "And no whining!"

You Might Be a Cowgirl If

. . . you can drink your coffee any way but weak.

. . . at least one of the stations on your car radio is programmed to a country-western station.

. . . you think playing with horses is better than playing with your kids or grandkids.

7

THE TRAIL AHEAD

It's the way you ride the trail that counts.
—Dale Evans

A cowgirl has to gallop fast and work a big lasso to achieve her goals. She knows that when the riding gets rough, you tilt your hat down, use your spurs, and get tough. A cowgirl knows that when life bucks you off, you just have to dust yourself off, cowgirl up, and get back in the saddle. Wisdom is realizing you're riding down the wrong trail (again), and knowing that you can turn around and retrace your steps to find the right trail to follow. To fly, you only need to take the reins and go. And when it comes to life's adventures, never pull back on the reins.

Whether you've always known your inner cowgirl or whether you're rediscovering your long-lost cowgirl self, you know life can be a long and often exhausting trail, with steep slopes, rocky terrain, raging rivers to cross, breathtaking views at the top, and then another slide down into an unmapped valley. Always remember that you can take the support and advice from other smart cowgirls along with you on the ride. I hope that it will be a rewarding and fulfilling journey for you.

Happy trails!

RESOURCES FOR OUTFITTING YOUR LIFE ON THE RANGE

All Things Horses and More

http://horsecity.com

Classified ads, blogs, articles, photos, and stories—this is a horse lover's dream site.

American Cowgirl, Connie Reeves: Always Saddle Your Own Horse

www.youtube.com/watch?v=6P6aJ7h8uLc&feature=related

This video, shot by my friend Jamie Williams, is a must-see. Connie Reeves appears here shortly before her death at one hundred years young.

Artwork and More

www.zazzle.com/CowgirlCafeOnline

This gallery features truly unique vintage and retro Western designs, organized by a variety of art themes. Within each theme you will find a number of items to purchase for your own home or ranch decor, or as terrific gift items for your fellow cowgirls.

At the Movies: Dude Ranch Fashions

www.britishpathe.com/record.php?id=56283

Visit this site to see the film of 1940s cowgirl fashion, mentioned in chapter 5.

Cowgirls and Indians Resale

161 E. Cascade Avenue
Sisters, OR 97759
(541) 549-6950
www.cowgirlresale.com

Gently used cowgirl apparel, boots, bags, and turquoise jewelry, to buy or sell. Give Kate Aspen a call!

Cowgirl U

www.janmendoza.com

This is where you can get it all together, as well as go to Cowgirl U, learn to trick-ride, or just spend some time hanging out with this terrific cowgirl.

Crow's Nest Trading Company

3205 Airport Boulevard NW
Wilson, NC 27896
(800) 325-9897
www.crowsnesttrading.com

This is where you will find that one special piece (or several pieces) to proclaim your cowgirl decor spirit. Unique clothing, too! Be sure to request a catalog.

Find Your Brand!

www.steakbrandingirons.com/mini-small-steak-branding-irons.php

This is where you can order a custom brand, or ones that are already designed and ready for purchase.

Follow Your Dreams: Gold Dog Consulting

www.golddogconsulting.com

Cindy Hooker (management coaching, teambuilding, and facilitation) is prepared to help you ride herd on your dreams.

Glitzy Girls Western Wear

www.rodeoqueenclothesonline.com

Your rodeo queen outfit awaits you here! Custom designs, made by hand. Even if you aren't going for the crown, you'll enjoy these designs.

Let There Be Light—But Western

www.thestoeckleincollection.com

Happy to say that Stoecklein Photography has put some of their best Western-style photos on lampshades!

Music to Your Ears

www.rangeradio.com

Range Radio features a traditional roots–based classic country musical format with a modern "trail mix" of old and new Western music artists. Range Radio is fun, and is designed to surprise listeners with artists such as Merle Haggard, Patsy Cline, Willie Nelson, Bob Wills, George Strait, Chris LeDoux, Asleep at the Wheel, Lyle Lovett, Robert Earl Keen, Ian Tyson, Don Edwards, Dave Stamey, Joni Harms, Eliza Gilkyson, Norah Jones, Marty Robbins, R. W. Hampton, Michael Martin Murphy, Rex Allen, Gene Autry, Roy Rogers, Tom Hiatt, Tom Russell, Patty Griffin, Nanci Griffith, Neil Young, Kevin Costner, Jeff Bridges, Mark Knopfler, Emmylou Harris, and many more.

Nancy Becker: Cowgirl True

www.nancybeckerstudio.com, www.remembranceartglassmemorials.com, and www.theintuitiveforce.com

Nancy Becker is the owner and founder of Nancy Becker Studio. She is dedicated to assisting women discover, claim, and engage their infinite soul potential and become familiar with their own sense of *Cowgirl True*.

Pillow Talk

www.luckystargallery.com

This is a great Western-style, one-of-a-kind shopping site for custom-made pillows and more that speak of cowgirls and the Old West.

Sisters of the Silver Sage

www.sistersofthesilversage.com

Donna and her sisters, Rhonda and Janet, are the Sisters of the Silver Sage. They live in the foothills of the Great Smoky Mountains, and their hearts are in the American West. Some say they sound like female Sons of the Pioneers, with just a touch of the Andrews Sisters and the McGuire Sisters. Rhonda sings a sparkling, true lead; Janet sings high tenor while playing the electric bass guitar; and Donna comes in with alto harmonies and some lead vocals. They have performed on stages throughout the Southeast as well as Las Vegas, Nevada, and Branson, Missouri. Visit their website to sample their music, buy their albums, or visit their "Wildwood Ranch," their home in the hills via the Internet, to read about their latest adventures.

Western Shirts and More

www.rockmount.com

If you want a really great Western shirt, then check out this site. Rockmount Ranch Wear invented the snap on the Western shirt, and you can't get more authentic than that! Roy Rogers wore them, and many movie stars wear their shirts today. If you are in downtown Denver, stop by and visit their retail store and small museum.

Wild Rags

www.buckaroobrand.com

Buckaroo Brand Wild Rags are made by Amy Mundell in Crane, Oregon. Amy knows buckaroos and what they like. Her wild rags are made from many kinds of fabric, sometimes vintage, and only a limited amount is made of any one fabric. If you are after an authentic addition to your own personal cowgirl style, you'll find it here.

BIBLIOGRAPHY

Brown, Corinne Joy. *Come and Get It: The Saga of Western Dinnerware.* Boulder, CO: Johnson Books, 2011.

Burbick, Joan. *Rodeo Queens: On the Circuit with America's Cowgirls.* New York: PublicAffairs / Perseus Books Group, 2002.

Jordan, Teresa. *Cowgirls: Women of the American West.* Lincoln, Nebraska and London, England: University of Nebraska Press, 1992.

Mendoza, Jan. *I Was Born To Be: A Guide to Fulfilling Your Lifelong Dreams.* Far West Publishing, 2009.

Rauch, Jamie. *Rodeo Queen University: Teach the Teachers—A Guide for Rodeo Queen Committees.* Self-published, 2010.

Smith, Ellen Reid. *Cowgirl Smarts: How to Rope a Kick-Ass Life.* Austin, TX: Reid Smith & Associates, Inc., 2007.

Turnbaugh, Kay. *The Last of the Wild West Cowgirls.* Nederland, CO: Perigo Press, 2009.

ABOUT THE AUTHOR

Jill Charlotte Stanford's lifelong ambition has been to be a cowgirl. She has owned and ridden horses all her life, competing in major horse shows as well as gathering cattle out on the range. She has known the joy of galloping her horse through the surf on the beaches of Oregon. She has sailed over jumps and has held a newborn foal in her arms. She feels that the best part of writing her books is the connections she has made with cowgirls all over the United States. "I stand in awe of these tough yet gentle women," she says. "I am honored that they think I am a cowgirl too." Jill lives and writes in Sisters, Oregon.

From the author's collection

ABOUT THE PHOTOGRAPHER

*To me, photography is an art of observation. It's about
finding something interesting in an ordinary place . . .
I've found it has little to do with the things you see and
everything to do with the way you see them.*

—Elliott Erwitt

Robin L. Corey is a photographer who makes her home in Washington State's Central Basin desert area. Acquainted with ranch and rodeo for more than twenty-five years, Western images and lifestyle remain her primary interest for subject matter. Her grandchildren and beloved bay mare are favorites when it comes to how she likes to spend her free time.

Photo by Mary McConnell Roberts